Exploring Earth's Resources

Using Coal, Oil, and Gas

Sharon Katz Cooper

Heinemann Library
Chicago, Illinois

Designed by Michelle Lisseter
Printed and bound in China, by South China Printing Company

11 10 09 08 07
10 9 8 7 6 5 4 3 2 1

Library of Congress Cataloging-in-Publication Data

Katz Cooper, Sharon.
  Using coal, oil, and gas / Sharon Katz Cooper.
      p. cm. -- (Exploring Earth's resources)
  Includes index.
  ISBN-13: 978-1-4034-9318-7 (lib. bdg.)
  ISBN-10: 1-4034-9318-9 (lib. bdg.)
  ISBN-13: 978-1-4034-9326-2 (pbk.)
  ISBN-10: 1-4034-9326-X (pbk.)
 1. Coal--Juvenile literature. 2. Petroleum--Juvenile literature. 3. Natural gas--Juvenile
literature. I. Title.
  TN801.K38 2007
  553.2--dc22

                                                    2006029704

Acknowledgments
The publishers would like to thank the following for permission to reproduce photographs:
Alamy pp. 14 (Marie-Louise Avery), 18 (PHOTOTAKE Inc.), 19 (Horizon International Images
Limited); Corbis pp. 9 (SABA/Peter Blakely), 11 (Royalty Free), 12 (Paul A. Souders), 17, 21
(Royalty Free), 21 (Mango Productions); Getty p. 22 (Photodisc); Harcourt Education p. 13
(Tudor Photography); Jupiter p. 5 (Banana Stock); Rex Features p. 15; Science Photo Library
& istock & Getty Images p. 4 (Photodisc); Still pictures pp. 8 (UNEP/S.Compoint), 10 (Peter
Frischmuth), 16 (Jochen Tack/Das Fotoarchiv), 20 (Jeff Greenberg).

Cover photograph reproduced with permission of Alamy (Mark Sykes).

Every effort has been made to contact copyright holders of any material reproduced in
this book. Any omissions will be rectified in subsequent printings if notice is given to the
publishers.

Contents

What Are Coal, Oil, and Natural Gas? . 4

What Are Coal, Oil, and Gas Made Of? 6

How Do We Find Coal, Oil, and Gas? . . 8

How Do We Use Coal, Oil, and Gas? . 12

Who Studies Coal, Oil, and Gas? 18

Will We Ever Run Out of Coal, Oil,

   and Gas? 20

Fueling Electricity 22

Glossary. 23

Index 24

Some words are shown in bold, **like this**.
You can find them in the glossary on page 23.

What Are Coal, Oil, and Natural Gas?

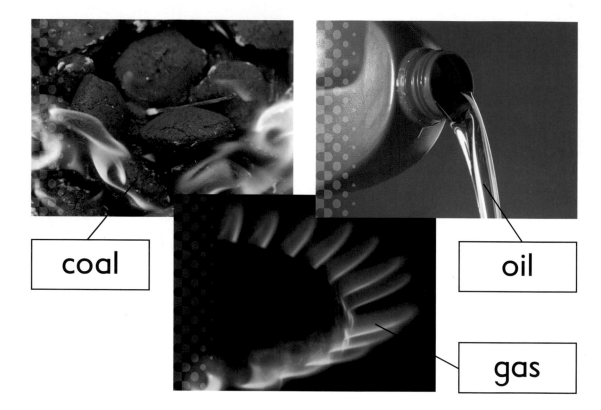

coal

oil

gas

Coal, oil, and natural gas are **natural resources**.

Natural resources come from Earth.

Coal, oil, and natural gas are fuels.

We use fuels for **energy**.

What Are Coal, Oil, and Gas Made Of?

①

rotting trees

mud

Coal, oil, and natural gas are **fossil fuels**.

They are the remains of plants and animals that lived long ago.

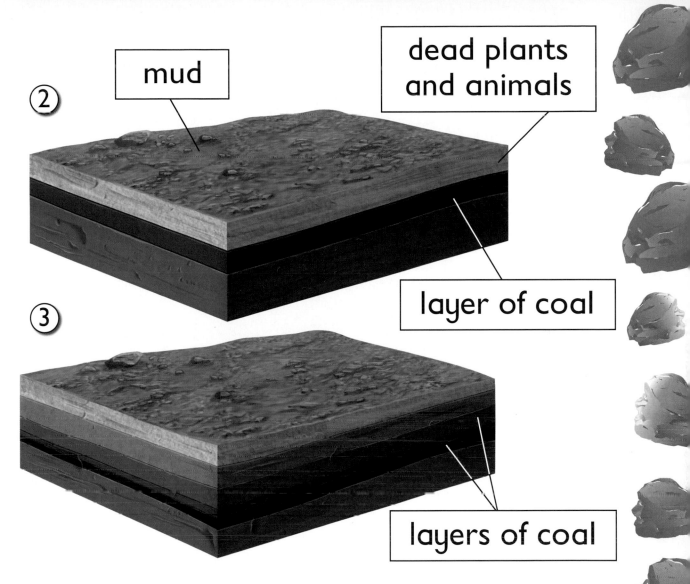

② mud

dead plants and animals

layer of coal

③ layers of coal

Thick mud covered these plants and animals after they died.

After a long time, they turned into coal, oil, or gas.

How Do We Find Coal, Oil, and Gas?

oil

We find **fossil fuels** deep underground.

We drill deep into Earth. We pump out oil and natural gas.

Ships and big pipes move oil and natural gas.

They take the fossil fuels to places where we can use them.

Coal is also found deep underground.

When scientists find a place with a lot of coal, workers dig a **mine**.

Miners go deep into the ground and cut out the coal.

Special trains bring the coal up to the surface.

How Do We Use Coal, Oil, and Gas?

Power plants burn coal, oil, and gas to make electricity.

We use this electricity to light houses, schools, and workplaces.

We also use **fossil fuels** to make plastics.

Many of the objects you use every day are made from plastic.

13

Some homes use natural gas for cooking and heating.

The gas burns with a blue flame.

Many people around the world
burn coal for heating and cooking.

We use gas, oil, and coal to help us get around.

Many trains and airplanes use diesel fuel. Diesel is a type of oil.

Most cars run on gasoline.

Gasoline is also made from oil.

17

Who Studies Coal, Oil, and Gas?

Scientists who study rocks are called **geologists**.

They look for new places to drill for oil and gas.

Engineers look for the safest ways to get fuels out of the ground.

Will We Ever Run Out of Coal, Oil, and Gas?

Fossil fuels are **non-renewable**.

Once we use them up, they will be gone forever.

To make fossil fuels last longer, we can use bikes instead of cars.

We can use different kinds of **energy**, like wind power.

Fueling Electricity

We use **fossil fuels** to make electricity. Look at this picture. Which objects use electricity? Which objects use gas? Can you think of four ways you could use less electricity at home?

Glossary

 **energy** something that gives power

 **engineer** scientist who knows how to make and fix machines

 **fossil fuel** gas, oil, or coal. Fossil fuels are made from plants and animals that lived long ago.

 **geologist** scientist who studies rocks

 **mine** place in the ground where coal is found

 **natural resource** material from Earth that we can use

 **non-renewable** something that will not last forever and will run out one day

23

Index

cooking   14, 15

diesel   16

drill   8, 18, 19

electricity   12, 22

fossil fuels   6–9, 13, 20–22

gasoline   17

heating   14, 15

mines   10, 11

pipes   9

plastics   13

power plants   12

transportation   5, 16, 17, 21

wind power   21